I Can
Multiply and Divide

Send all inquiries to:
School Specialty Publishing
8720 Orion Place
Columbus, OH 43240-2111

ISBN 0-7696-2917-2

9 10 HPS 11 10 09

Name _____

9-column ↓

×	0	1	2	3	4	5	6	7	8	9
0	0	0	0	0	0	0	0	0	0	0
1	0	1	2	3	4	5	6	7	8	9
2	0	2	4	6	8	10	12	14	16	18
3	0	3	6	9	12	15	18	21	24	27
4	0	4	8	12	16	20	24	28	32	36
5	0	5	10	15	20	25	30	35	40	45
6	0	6	12	18	24	30	36	42	48	54
7	0	7	14	21	28	35	42	49	56	63
8	0	8	16	24	32	40	48	56	64	72
9	0	9	18	27	36	45	54	63	72	(81)

9-row

$$\begin{array}{r} 9 \\ \times\ 9 \\ \hline 81 \end{array}$$

9 ⟶ Find the 9-row.

× 9 ⟶ Find the 9-column.

81 ⟵ The product is named where the 9-row and 9-column meet.

Multiplication

Multiply.

Name _____

$$\begin{array}{r} 3 \\ \times\ 5 \\ \hline \end{array} \qquad \begin{array}{r} 7 \\ \times\ 4 \\ \hline \end{array} \qquad \begin{array}{r} 2 \\ \times\ 1 \\ \hline \end{array} \qquad \begin{array}{r} 7 \\ \times\ 5 \\ \hline \end{array} \qquad \begin{array}{r} 8 \\ \times\ 8 \\ \hline \end{array} \qquad \begin{array}{r} 8 \\ \times\ 9 \\ \hline \end{array}$$

$$\begin{array}{r} 5 \\ \times\ 3 \\ \hline \end{array} \qquad \begin{array}{r} 6 \\ \times\ 7 \\ \hline \end{array} \qquad \begin{array}{r} 1 \\ \times\ 1 \\ \hline \end{array} \qquad \begin{array}{r} 7 \\ \times\ 4 \\ \hline \end{array} \qquad \begin{array}{r} 8 \\ \times\ 4 \\ \hline \end{array} \qquad \begin{array}{r} 7 \\ \times\ 5 \\ \hline \end{array}$$

$$\begin{array}{r} 9 \\ \times\ 0 \\ \hline \end{array} \qquad \begin{array}{r} 5 \\ \times\ 8 \\ \hline \end{array} \qquad \begin{array}{r} 8 \\ \times\ 6 \\ \hline \end{array} \qquad \begin{array}{r} 7 \\ \times\ 7 \\ \hline \end{array}$$

Multiplication

Multiply.

Name _____

| 5 | 2 | 6 | 7 | 9 | 0 |
| x 4 | x 1 | x 4 | x 9 | x 6 | x 0 |

| 8 | 4 | 8 | 4 | 3 | 6 |
| x 7 | x 2 | x 5 | x 3 | x 8 | x 3 |

| 7 | 5 | 8 | 9 |
| x 7 | x 9 | x 5 | x 1 |

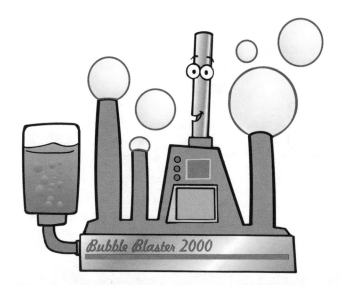

Bubble Blaster 2000

Multiply.

Name _____

```
   2          7          7          8          8          2
 x 6        x 4        x 5        x 0        x 5        x 7
```

```
   6          5          5          9          8          6
 x 7        x 8        x 2        x 9        x 3        x 6
```

```
   8          3          5          7
 x 0        x 5        x 1        x 9
```

Multiplication

Multiply.

Name _____

4	7	8	9	9	6
x 2	x 5	x 6	x 7	x 0	x 3

5	7	5	6	7	6
x 7	x 1	x 6	x 0	x 7	x 4

7	2	6	5
x 3	x 3	x 2	x 3

Multiply.

Name _____

```
    4          7          3          8          9          0
  x 6        x 5        x 8        x 6        x 9        x 0
```

```
    4          8          6          4          6          5
  x 7        x 5        x 4        x 7        x 6        x 4
```

```
    7          5          1          4
  x 0        x 3        x 1        x 2
```

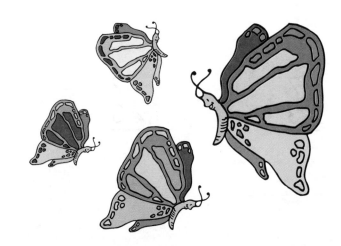

Multiplication
✖

Multiply.

Name _____

5 x 1 =   5 x 3 =   7 x 7 =   8 x 5 =   3 x 3 =

6 x 4 =   5 x 7 =   4 x 2 =   1 x 1 =   6 x 9 =

3 x 1 =   3 x 3 =   5 x 8 =   4 x 7 =   5 x 5 =

6 x 6 =   7 x 4 =   6 x 4 =

Multiply.

Name _____

5 x 3 =   2 x 1 =   3 x 8 =   6 x 5 =   3 x 6 =

6 x 6 =   4 x 7 =   4 x 2 =   4 x 3 =   5 x 8 =

4 x 4 =   3 x 0 =   7 x 7 =   7 x 0 =   3 x 3 =

3 x 9 =   7 x 5 =   2 x 8 =

Multiplication

Multiply.

Name _____

$2 \times 1 =$ $4 \times 4 =$ $7 \times 5 =$ $4 \times 0 =$ $8 \times 3 =$

$1 \times 1 =$ $0 \times 5 =$ $3 \times 2 =$ $7 \times 7 =$ $8 \times 5 =$

$1 \times 8 =$ $8 \times 5 =$ $4 \times 9 =$ $5 \times 3 =$ $4 \times 6 =$

$6 \times 6 =$ $5 \times 5 =$ $4 \times 0 =$

Multiplication

Multiply.

Name _____

8 x 4 =

6 x 8 =

7 x 3 =

0 x 6 =

3 x 2 =

5 x 3 =

6 x 2 =

1 x 8 =

5 x 7 =

7 x 7 =

9 x 5 =

7 x 8 =

8 x 4 =

7 x 4 =

5 x 5 =

0 x 4 =

2 x 2 =

9 x 2 =

Multiplication

✖

Multiply.

Name _____

$8 \times 4 =$ $3 \times 7 =$ $5 \times 9 =$ $7 \times 6 =$ $2 \times 1 =$

$3 \times 3 =$ $7 \times 0 =$ $3 \times 8 =$ $4 \times 4 =$ $8 \times 8 =$

$1 \times 1 =$ $6 \times 3 =$ $0 \times 0 =$ $7 \times 9 =$ $7 \times 2 =$

$4 \times 9 =$ $5 \times 5 =$ $2 \times 0 =$

Multiplication
✕

Multiply.

Name _____

1 x 1 =

7 x 0 =

4 x 4 =

3 x 8 =

7 x 5 =

8 x 4 =

2 x 7 =

4 x 3 =

1 x 0 =

2 x 4 =

7 x 4 =

3 x 3 =

9 x 6 =

5 x 5 =

6 x 3 =

1 x 7 =

3 x 7 =

6 x 0 =

Multiplication

Multiply.

Name _____

$5 \times 3 =$ $8 \times 9 =$ $1 \times 0 =$ $7 \times 4 =$ $0 \times 0 =$

$$
\begin{array}{r} 3 \\ \times\ 7 \\ \hline \end{array}
\qquad
\begin{array}{r} 7 \\ \times\ 7 \\ \hline \end{array}
\qquad
\begin{array}{r} 4 \\ \times\ 8 \\ \hline \end{array}
\qquad
\begin{array}{r} 9 \\ \times\ 5 \\ \hline \end{array}
\qquad
\begin{array}{r} 3 \\ \times\ 3 \\ \hline \end{array}
\qquad
\begin{array}{r} 6 \\ \times\ 9 \\ \hline \end{array}
$$

$1 \times 5 =$ $6 \times 4 =$ $2 \times 8 =$

15

Multiply.

Name _____

$6 \times 3 =$ $3 \times 9 =$ $7 \times 7 =$ $5 \times 9 =$ $6 \times 0 =$

$$\begin{array}{r} 3 \\ \times\, 7 \\ \hline \end{array} \qquad \begin{array}{r} 8 \\ \times\, 8 \\ \hline \end{array} \qquad \begin{array}{r} 4 \\ \times\, 7 \\ \hline \end{array} \qquad \begin{array}{r} 8 \\ \times\, 9 \\ \hline \end{array} \qquad \begin{array}{r} 9 \\ \times\, 0 \\ \hline \end{array} \qquad \begin{array}{r} 5 \\ \times\, 5 \\ \hline \end{array}$$

$1 \times 1 =$ $6 \times 7 =$ $8 \times 5 =$

Multiplication Word Problems

Multiplication ✖

Solve each problem.

Name _____

Yesterday, Ken saw 2 birds.

Today, he sees 3 times as many.

How many birds did he see today?

$$\begin{array}{r} 2 \\ \times\ 3 \\ \hline 6 \end{array}$$

Yesterday, Ben had 4 pencils.

Today, he has 2 times as many.

How many pencils does he have today?

Rachel had 1 rabbit.

Today, she gets 9 times more rabbits.

How many rabbits are there today?

Patty ran 2 miles.

Today, she ran 3 times as many miles.

How many miles did she run today?

Multiplication Word Problems

Solve each problem.

Name _____

Molly had 7 marbles.

She came home with 2 times as many.

X

How many marbles does she have now?

Chris did 4 experiments last year.

This year he did 2 times as many.

X

How many did he do this year?

Doug has 2 toys.

He got 3 times as many for his birthday.

X

How many toys did he get?

Clyde ran 8 laps yesterday.

Today he ran 3 times as many.

X

How many laps did he run today?

Multiplication Word Problems

Solve each problem.

Name _____

Keith sings 3 songs on Monday.

He sings 3 times as many on Tuesday.

How many songs does Keith sing on Tuesday?

X [ ]

Roger has 2 coats.

Ben has 4 times as many coats.

How many coats does Ben have?

X [ ]

Beth has 8 dolls.

Paige has 1 times as many.

How many dolls does Paige have?

X [ ]

Chris had 3 cards.

He comes home with 2 times as many.

How many cards does he have now?

X [ ]

Multiplication

X

Solve each problem.

Name _____

Yesterday, Lindsay saw 4 butterflies.

She saw 7 times more today.

X

How many butterflies did she see today?

Jill did 5 pushups yesterday.

She did 5 times more today.

X

How many pushups did she do today?

There are 4 people in Tom's family.

Sam has 2 times as many in his family.

X

How many people are in Sam's family?

Dennis sees 8 cars.

Yesterday, he saw 3 times as many.

X

How many cars were there yesterday?

Multiplication Word Problems

Multiplication ✗

Solve each problem.

Name _____

Kevin is 3 feet tall.

His dad is 2 times as tall as Kevin.

How tall is Kevin's dad?

Stuart drinks 7 glasses of water.

Yesterday, he drank 2 times as many.

How many glasses did he drink yesterday?

Emily drew 2 houses yesterday.

Today she drew 4 times as many.

How many houses did she draw today?

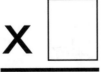

Sarah fixed 2 lamps yesterday.

Today she fixed 8 times as many.

How many lamps did she fix today?

Multiplication Word Problems

Solve each problem.

Name _____

Dorthy saw 5 kites yesterday.

She saw 8 times more kites today.

How many kites did she see today?

Ben has 2 toys.

Today he has 7 times more toys.

How many toys does Ben have?

Brenda has 2 children.

Her sister has 2 times as many children.

How many children does her sister have?

Yesterday Katie has 2 bottles.

Today, she has 3 times as many bottles.

How many bottles does Katie have?

Multiplication

Multiply.

Name _____

```
  6 4        2 6        9 6        1 3        4 2        3 4
x   8      x   7      x   0      x   5      x   6      x   2
```

```
  2 8        2 4        7 4        5 5        9 0        4 5
x   5      x   3      x   8      x   4      x   5      x   2
```

```
  6 0        6 3        2 1        8 4
x   7      x   6      x   5      x   0
```

Multiply.

Name _____

73 x 2	28 x 5	68 x 3	10 x 5	42 x 7	32 x 9
63 x 5	21 x 7	84 x 5	38 x 6	48 x 4	31 x 8
16 x 2	35 x 9	11 x 1	64 x 8		

Multiplication

Name _____

Multiply.

```
  6 5        7 3        8 4        4 3        7 0        9 2
x   4      x   1      x   3      x   2      x   5      x   1
```

```
  5 3        8 5        8 4        9 5        7 4        8 4
x   2      x   6      x   2      x   2      x   1      x   3
```

```
  3 1        6 3        4 3        7 5
x   5      x   1      x   7      x   4
```

Multiply.

Name _____

```
  7 3          3 5          1 1          8 4          9 6          4 2
x   5        x   2        x   7        x   3        x   7        x   7
_____        _____        _____        _____        _____        _____


  6 4          3 4          6 5          4 5          3 2          7 4
x   5        x   7        x   9        x   8        x   7        x   7
_____        _____        _____        _____        _____        _____


  1 3          5 3          7 4          7 1
x   6        x   7        x   5        x   0
_____        _____        _____        _____
```

Multiply.

Name _____

```
  4 2          1 6          4 7          3 7          8 5          6 4
x   6        x   2        x   8        x   9        x   6        x   7
_____     _____     _____     _____     _____     _____
```

```
  3 2          5 1          7 5          2 1          7 4          1 7
x   7        x   2        x   6        x   4        x   5        x   5
_____     _____     _____     _____     _____     _____
```

```
  6 4          4 2          7 5          9 5
x   7        x   7        x   3        x   1
_____     _____     _____     _____
```

Multiplication

Multiply.

Name _____

32 x 7	74 x 5	83 x 1	42 x 7	40 x 6	91 x 1
33 x 1	53 x 0	47 x 5	83 x 8	42 x 7	79 x 2
64 x 8	31 x 6	85 x 4	43 x 1		

Multiplication

Multiply.

Name ____________________

14 x 4 =	15 x 8 =	76 x 3 =	62 x 8 =	58 x 0 =
52 x 1 =	97 x 6 =	95 x 1 =	57 x 7 =	62 x 4 =
81 x 3 =	72 x 2 =	82 x 1 =	10 x 9 =	86 x 5 =
84 x 5 =	58 x 3 =	76 x 4 =		

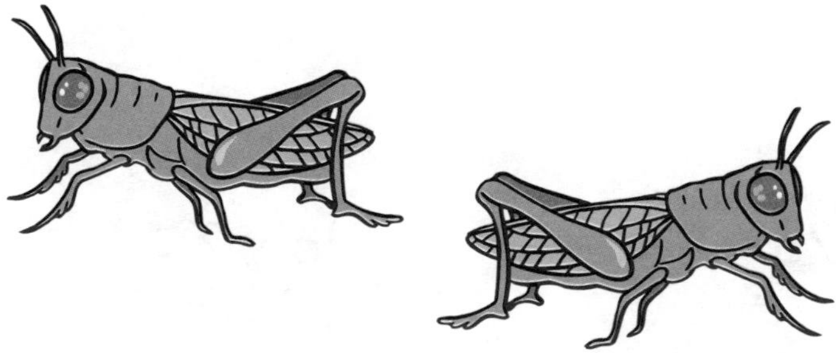

Multiply.

Name _____

25 x 1 =   75 x 4 =   79 x 7 =   13 x 3 =   78 x 8 =

83 x 1 =   18 x 0 =   47 x 8 =   30 x 1 =   91 x 7 =

15 x 4 =   82 x 1 =   19 x 8 =   46 x 0 =   58 x 3 =

76 x 8 =   46 x 7 =   49 x 6 =

Multiplication

✖

Multiply.

Name _____

48 x 7 =   29 x 6 =   92 x 4 =   63 x 0 =   36 x 8 =

22 x 1 =   19 x 9 =   57 x 2 =   10 x 3 =   85 x 6 =

83 x 6 =   59 x 3 =   82 x 1 =   39 x 5 =   60 x 1 =

11 x 4 =   55 x 3 =   95 x 9 =

Multiplication ✖

Multiply.

Name _____

$37 \times 1 =$ $84 \times 1 =$ $69 \times 7 =$ $48 \times 8 =$ $46 \times 2 =$

$83 \times 7 =$ $60 \times 4 =$ $22 \times 6 =$ $10 \times 6 =$ $62 \times 4 =$

$90 \times 1 =$ $59 \times 2 =$ $43 \times 5 =$ $73 \times 2 =$ $10 \times 1 =$

$68 \times 5 =$ $93 \times 0 =$ $10 \times 7 =$

Multiply.

Name _____

48 x 1 =   83 x 5 =   74 x 5 =   46 x 0 =   18 x 6 =

57 x 8 =   48 x 2 =   83 x 7 =   75 x 7 =   49 x 8 =

55 x 2 =   88 x 3 =   74 x 0 =   24 x 1 =   92 x 8 =

46 x 4 =   76 x 7 =   84 x 8 =

Multiply.

97 x 4 =   62 x 6 =   10 x 7 =   76 x 3 =   73 x 5 =

19 x 1 =   33 x 4 =   16 x 0 =   70 x 7 =   72 x 2 =

18 x 4 =   43 x 7 =   49 x 7 =   55 x 3 =   15 x 5 =

54 x 7 =   72 x 6 =   36 x 8 =

Multiply.

Name _____

$67 \times 3 =$ $19 \times 5 =$ $49 \times 9 =$ $76 \times 1 =$ $28 \times 7 =$

$$\begin{array}{r} 3\ 6 \\ \times\ \ 5 \\ \hline \end{array}$$
$$\begin{array}{r} 9\ 5 \\ \times\ \ 1 \\ \hline \end{array}$$
$$\begin{array}{r} 5\ 0 \\ \times\ \ 6 \\ \hline \end{array}$$
$$\begin{array}{r} 1\ 4 \\ \times\ \ 3 \\ \hline \end{array}$$
$$\begin{array}{r} 3\ 9 \\ \times\ \ 4 \\ \hline \end{array}$$
$$\begin{array}{r} 2\ 7 \\ \times\ \ 0 \\ \hline \end{array}$$

$76 \times 6 =$ $59 \times 4 =$ $43 \times 1 =$

Multiply.

Name _____

84 x 1 =   29 x 4 =   17 x 0 =   57 x 7 =   33 x 3 =

```
   47            13            64            85            52            14
x   9         x   6         x   2         x   0         x   7         x   7
```

46 x 7 =   28 x 5 =   43 x 8 =

Multiplication
X

Solve each problem.

Name _____

Andy had 39 cards yesterday.

Today, he got 2 times more cards.

$$\begin{array}{r} 39 \\ \times\ 2 \\ \hline 78 \end{array}$$

How many cards does he have today?

Beth saw 29 bees yesterday.

Today she saw 8 times more bees.

How many bees are there today?

Sammy hit 11 homeruns last year.

He hit 5 times that many this year.

How many homeruns did he hit this year?

Last year, Al won 32 games.

He won 2 times that this year.

How many games did he win?

Multiplication Word Problems

Solve each problem.

Name _____

Pam ran 14 miles.

Jill ran 5 times more than Pam.

X

How many miles did Jill run?

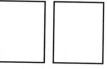

Luke has 42 toy cars.

His brother has 3 times more.

X

How many does he have?

Tiffany saw 50 trees yesterday.

Today she saw 7 times as many.

X

How many trees did she see today?

Devon caught 13 fish.

Lori caught 4 times as many.

X

How many fish did Lori catch?

Multiplication X

Solve each problem.

Name _____

Today, Pam sold 14 baskets.

She sold 8 times as many yesterday.

How many did she sell yesterday?

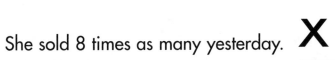

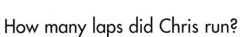

Greg ran 37 laps.

Chris ran 7 times as many laps.

How many laps did Chris run?

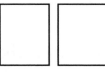
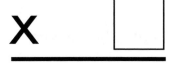

Last year, Ben read 41 books.

He read 2 times as many this year.

How many books did he read?

Dorthy has 12 ribbons.

Amy has 3 times as many.

How many ribbons does Amy have?

Multiplication Word Problems

Solve each problem.

Name _____

Fred scored 19 touchdowns.

Tim scored 3 times more than Fred.

How many touchdowns did Tim score?

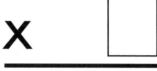

Doug ran 41 laps.

Pam ran 5 times as long.

How many laps did Pam run?

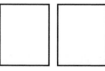

Bob went to school with 31 marbles.

He came home with 6 times more.

How many marbles does Bob have?

Rachel danced for 10 hours.

Jill danced for 2 times as long.

How many hours did Jill dance?

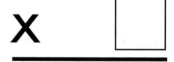

Multiplication Word Problems

Multiplication
X

Solve each problem.

Name _____

Brad has 10 cats.

Kelsey has 5 times as many cats.

How many cats does Kelsey have?

$$\begin{array}{r} \square\;\square \\ \times \quad \square \\ \hline \square\;\square \end{array}$$

Mark sang 28 songs yesterday.

He sang 1 times as many today.

How many songs did he sing today?

$$\begin{array}{r} \square\;\square \\ \times \quad \square \\ \hline \square\;\square \end{array}$$

Ted saw 29 boats yesterday.

He saw 7 times as many today.

How many boats were there today?

$$\begin{array}{r} \square\;\square \\ \times \quad \square \\ \hline \square\;\square\;\square \end{array}$$

Emily has 12 puppies.

Amy has 4 times as many.

How many puppies does Amy have?

$$\begin{array}{r} \square\;\square \\ \times \quad \square \\ \hline \square\;\square \end{array}$$

Multiplication Word Problems

Solve each problem.

Name _____

Ted has 47 cds.

Pam has 2 times as many.

How many cds does Pam have?

Rachel slept for 11 hours.

Janet slept for 2 times as long.

How many hours did Janet sleep?

Julie taught 23 students.

Molly taught 3 times as many.

How many students did Molly teach?

Kyle has 72 books.

Erin has 2 times as many.

How many books does Erin have?

Multiply.

Name _____

$84 \times 5 =$ $7 \times 1 =$ $43 \times 0 =$ $5 \times 7 =$ $61 \times 7 =$

$$\begin{array}{r} 3\ 6 \\ \times\ \ 4 \\ \hline \end{array}$$
$$\begin{array}{r} 1 \\ \times\ 1 \\ \hline \end{array}$$
$$\begin{array}{r} 7\ 4 \\ \times\ \ 3 \\ \hline \end{array}$$
$$\begin{array}{r} 9 \\ \times\ 6 \\ \hline \end{array}$$
$$\begin{array}{r} 4\ 2 \\ \times\ \ 1 \\ \hline \end{array}$$
$$\begin{array}{r} 8 \\ \times\ 5 \\ \hline \end{array}$$

$4 \times 3 =$ $94 \times 2 =$ $5 \times 7 =$

Multiplication Review

Multiply.

Name _____

95 x 3 =   7 x 0 =   38 x 1 =   8 x 4 =   91 x 6 =

```
   7 5            3              1 8             7            3 2              6
 x   5          x 7           x   6           x 4          x   9           x 0
```

9 x 9 =   67 x 1 =   8 x 5 =

Multiplication Review

Multiply.

Name _____

$94 \times 3 =$ $2 \times 7 =$ $47 \times 6 =$ $3 \times 6 =$ $49 \times 9 =$

$$
\begin{array}{r} 3\,5 \\ \times \quad 5 \\ \hline \end{array}
\qquad
\begin{array}{r} 0 \\ \times\, 8 \\ \hline \end{array}
\qquad
\begin{array}{r} 2\,5 \\ \times \quad 1 \\ \hline \end{array}
\qquad
\begin{array}{r} 4 \\ \times\, 6 \\ \hline \end{array}
\qquad
\begin{array}{r} 2\,7 \\ \times \quad 2 \\ \hline \end{array}
\qquad
\begin{array}{r} 6 \\ \times\, 8 \\ \hline \end{array}
$$

$4 \times 2 =$ $82 \times 3 =$ $6 \times 1 =$

Multiply.

Multiplication ✕

Name _____

25 x 7 =   2 x 6 =   57 x 1 =   9 x 8 =   63 x 4 =

```
   9 5              3              6 7              2              4 3              1
x    0           x  8           x    3           x  8           x    7           x  8
```

6 x 6 =   86 x 5 =   7 x 3 =

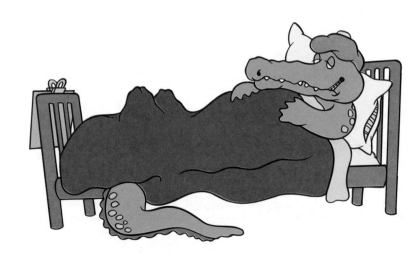

Multiplication Review

Multiply.

Name _____

76 x 5 =   7 x 6 =   59 x 7 =   1 x 5 =   56 x 9 =


```
  7 9          4          3 7          3          5 3          7
x   1        x 7        x   4        x 8        x   7        x 0
```

6 x 4 =   58 x 6 =   1 x 5 =

Multiplication Review

Multiply.

Name _____

59 x 3 =   2 x 7 =   57 x 4 =   8 x 1 =   93 x 6 =

$$\begin{array}{r} 3\ 7 \\ \times\ \ \ 5 \\ \hline \end{array}$$
$$\begin{array}{r} 2 \\ \times\ 7 \\ \hline \end{array}$$
$$\begin{array}{r} 7\ 4 \\ \times\ \ \ 6 \\ \hline \end{array}$$
$$\begin{array}{r} 5 \\ \times\ 2 \\ \hline \end{array}$$
$$\begin{array}{r} 7\ 4 \\ \times\ \ \ 5 \\ \hline \end{array}$$
$$\begin{array}{r} 1 \\ \times\ 9 \\ \hline \end{array}$$

0 x 7 =   27 x 4 =   6 x 2 =

Multiplication
✕

Multiply.

Name _____

$51 \times 3 =$ $8 \times 5 =$ $16 \times 6 =$ $7 \times 1 =$ $85 \times 4 =$

$$
\begin{array}{r}
47 \\
\times\ 6 \\
\hline
\end{array}
\qquad
\begin{array}{r}
0 \\
\times\ 5 \\
\hline
\end{array}
\qquad
\begin{array}{r}
15 \\
\times\ 3 \\
\hline
\end{array}
\qquad
\begin{array}{r}
7 \\
\times\ 4 \\
\hline
\end{array}
\qquad
\begin{array}{r}
74 \\
\times\ 8 \\
\hline
\end{array}
\qquad
\begin{array}{r}
9 \\
\times\ 6 \\
\hline
\end{array}
$$

$7 \times 3 =$ $13 \times 9 =$ $7 \times 3 =$

Multiplication Review

Multiply.

Name _____

19 x 5 =   7 x 8 =   28 x 1 =   7 x 4 =   53 x 0 =

```
   1 5             6             7 4             0            3 7              7
 x   4          x 3          x   8          x 5          x   5           x 1
 _____        _____        _____        _____        _____        _____
```

5 x 6 =   63 x 7 =   3 x 7 =

Multiplication Review

Multiplication

×

Multiply.

Name _____

71 x 5 =   7 x 7 =   43 x 9 =   8 x 4 =   86 x 8 =

```
   3 6            1              5 7              4              7 4              4
x    4         x 8           x    8          x 0           x    2          x 9
-------        -----         --------         -----         --------         -----
```

1 x 8 =   73 x 3 =   2 x 8 =

Multiplication Review

Multiply.

Name _____

76 x 1 =   4 x 4 =   29 x 7 =   8 x 3 =   82 x 7 =

```
  5 7          0            3 7          4            8 6            8
x   8        x 0          x   5        x 2          x   4          x 9
```

7 x 5 =   28 x 2 =   7 x 7 =

Multiplication
X

Multiply.

Name _____

64 x 3 =   7 x 3 =   72 x 1 =   9 x 9 =   49 x 6 =

```
    6 3          8          8 8          8          1 8          4
  x   7        x 5        x   1        x 4        x   9        x 3
```

7 x 0 =   58 x 1 =   8 x 7 =

Multiplication Review

Multiply.

Name _____

$85 \times 1 =$ $7 \times 7 =$ $28 \times 9 =$ $43 \times 3 =$ $53 \times 2 =$

$$\begin{array}{r} 53 \\ \times\ 7 \\ \hline \end{array}$$
$$\begin{array}{r} 3 \\ \times\ 8 \\ \hline \end{array}$$
$$\begin{array}{r} 78 \\ \times\ 5 \\ \hline \end{array}$$
$$\begin{array}{r} 8 \\ \times\ 5 \\ \hline \end{array}$$
$$\begin{array}{r} 30 \\ \times\ 6 \\ \hline \end{array}$$
$$\begin{array}{r} 4 \\ \times\ 8 \\ \hline \end{array}$$

$5 \times 1 =$ $91 \times 5 =$ $7 \times 7 =$

Multiply.

Name _____

73 x 1 =   0 x 7 =   57 x 9 =   7 x 6 =   43 x 2 =

```
   6 4            8             8 4            9            3 7             8
 x   1          x 4          x   9          x 0          x   5          x 9
```

8 x 1 =   19 x 6 =   3 x 8 =

Multiplication
✕

Multiply.

59 x 1 =   6 x 2 =   74 x 8 =   3 x 7 =   43 x 0 =

```
  3 7            7            6 8            3           1 1            5
x   5          x 8          x   3          x 6          x   0         x 8
```

7 x 1 =   67 x 5 =   9 x 0 =

Multiplication ✕

Solve each problem.

Name _____

Ken saw 2 birds yesterday.

He saw 3 times as many today.

X

How many birds did he see today?

Mary has 36 marbles.

She wins 2 times as many.

X

How many marbles did she win?

Ryan ran 13 laps yesterday.

Today, he ran 5 times as many.

X

How many laps did he run today?

Dave hit 5 homeruns.

Chris hit 2 times as many.

X

How many homeruns did Chris hit?

Multiplication ✖

Solve each problem.

Name _____

Beth has 2 pencils.

Rachel has 8 times as many.

How many colors does Rachel have?

X

Yesterday, Tim saw 47 ants.

Today, he saw 8 times as many.

How many ants did he see today?

X

Dennis had 87 cards.

Now he has 7 times as many.

How many cards does he have?

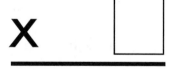
X

Lester teaches 4 classes.

Lucy teaches 1 times as many.

How many classes does Lucy teach?

X

Multiplication X

Solve each problem.

Name _____

Lori ran 3 laps yesterday.

Today, she ran 3 times as many laps.

X ☐
☐
_____
☐

How many laps did she run today?

Mark lives 58 miles from here.

Pam lives 5 times as far.

☐ ☐
X ☐
_____
☐ ☐ ☐

How many miles to Pam's house?

Penny ran 10 miles.

Emily ran 6 times as far.

☐ ☐
X ☐
_____
☐ ☐

How many miles did Emily run?

Kyle has 4 cousins.

Devon has 2 times as many.

☐
X ☐
_____
☐

How many cousins does Devon have?

Multiplication X

Solve each problem.

Name _____

Al has 9 dollars.

Keith has 0 times as many.

How many dollars does Keith have?

X

April has read 73 books.

Patty has read 4 times as many.

How many books has Patty read?

 X

Mark has 28 pencils.

Mary has 3 times as many.

How many pencils does Mary have?

 X

Barry has 4 sisters.

Pam has 1 times as many.

How many sisters does Pam have?

X

Multiplication
X

Solve each problem.

Name _____

Don has 2 cats.

Penny has 7 times more cats.

How many cats does Penny have?

X

Aaron ran 12 miles yesterday.

Today, he ran 3 times as many.

How many miles did Aaron run?

X

Tammy saw 15 ants yesterday.

She saw 6 times as many today.

How many ants did she see today?

X

Dan signed up for 4 classes.

Pam signed up for 3 times as many.

How many classes does Pam have?

X

Multiplication Word Problems Review

Solve each problem.

Name _____

Randy saw 2 movies.

Rob saw 1 times as many.

How many movies did Rob see?

$$\begin{array}{r} \square \\ \times\ \square \\ \hline \square \end{array}$$

Denise has 99 dolls.

Molly has 4 times as many.

How many dolls does Molly have?

$$\begin{array}{r} \square\ \square \\ \times\quad\ \square \\ \hline \square\ \square\ \square \end{array}$$

Kelly picked 38 flowers.

Sarah picked 3 times as many.

How many flowers did she pick?

$$\begin{array}{r} \square\ \square \\ \times\quad\ \square \\ \hline \square\ \square\ \square \end{array}$$

Dan slept for 4 hours.

Ralph slept for 2 times as long.

How many hours did Ralph sleep?

$$\begin{array}{r} \square \\ \times\ \square \\ \hline \square \end{array}$$

Division

Name _____

×	0	1	2	3	4	5	6	7	8	9
0	0	0	0	0	0	0	0	0	0	0
1	0	1	2	3	4	5	6	7	8	9
2	0	2	4	6	8	10	12	14	16	18
3	0	3	6	9	12	15	18	21	24	27
4	0	4	8	12	16	20	24	28	32	36
5	0	5	10	15	20	25	30	35	40	45
6	0	6	12	18	24	30	36	42	48	54
7	0	7	14	21	28	35	42	49	56	63
8	0	8	16	24	32	40	48	56	64	72
9	0	9	18	27	36	45	54	63	72	81

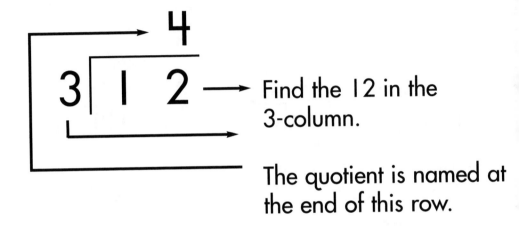

Find the 12 in the 3-column.

The quotient is named at the end of this row.

Division

Divide.

Name _____

$2\overline{)6}$ $3\overline{)9}$ $1\overline{)9}$ $4\overline{)8}$ $1\overline{)7}$ $2\overline{)8}$

$1\overline{)4}$ $3\overline{)6}$ $1\overline{)8}$ $3\overline{)9}$ $1\overline{)5}$ $4\overline{)8}$

$2\overline{)4}$ $9\overline{)9}$ $7\overline{)7}$ $1\overline{)7}$ $6\overline{)6}$ $2\overline{)6}$

$2\overline{)8}$ $3\overline{)9}$ $2\overline{)6}$ $4\overline{)8}$

Divide.

Name _____

$3\overline{)6}$ $9\overline{)9}$ $8\overline{)0}$ $4\overline{)8}$ $1\overline{)7}$ $3\overline{)9}$

$9\overline{)9}$ $2\overline{)2}$ $1\overline{)7}$ $3\overline{)3}$ $4\overline{)8}$ $7\overline{)7}$

$1\overline{)5}$ $2\overline{)4}$ $4\overline{)4}$ $5\overline{)5}$ $1\overline{)8}$ $6\overline{)6}$

$4\overline{)8}$ $1\overline{)6}$ $3\overline{)6}$ $2\overline{)8}$

Division

Divide.

Name _____

$1\overline{)4}$ $2\overline{)8}$ $7\overline{)7}$ $4\overline{)8}$ $7\overline{)0}$ $9\overline{)9}$

$4\overline{)8}$ $1\overline{)8}$ $3\overline{)9}$ $5\overline{)5}$ $1\overline{)6}$ $3\overline{)6}$

$3\overline{)3}$ $1\overline{)1}$ $4\overline{)4}$ $2\overline{)6}$ $3\overline{)9}$ $7\overline{)7}$

$2\overline{)8}$ $2\overline{)4}$ $4\overline{)4}$ $5\overline{)0}$

Divide.

Name _____

$1\overline{)9}$ $7\overline{)7}$ $5\overline{)5}$ $2\overline{)4}$ $2\overline{)8}$ $1\overline{)7}$

$3\overline{)6}$ $4\overline{)8}$ $1\overline{)5}$ $4\overline{)4}$ $9\overline{)9}$ $2\overline{)2}$

$1\overline{)5}$ $3\overline{)6}$ $1\overline{)1}$ $5\overline{)0}$ $4\overline{)8}$ $3\overline{)9}$

$1\overline{)4}$ $1\overline{)0}$ $5\overline{)5}$ $4\overline{)8}$

Division

Divide.

$2\overline{)2}$ $1\overline{)0}$ $4\overline{)8}$ $3\overline{)9}$ $2\overline{)8}$ $1\overline{)3}$

$4\overline{)4}$ $5\overline{)5}$ $1\overline{)7}$ $6\overline{)6}$ $7\overline{)0}$ $1\overline{)5}$

$2\overline{)8}$ $3\overline{)6}$ $4\overline{)8}$ $1\overline{)4}$ $7\overline{)7}$ $2\overline{)2}$

$1\overline{)8}$ $9\overline{)9}$ $4\overline{)8}$ $2\overline{)4}$

Division

Name _____

Divide.

$4 \div 4 =$ $8 \div 2 =$ $9 \div 1 =$ $0 \div 4 =$ $6 \div 3 =$

$5 \div 5 =$ $6 \div 3 =$ $9 \div 9 =$ $6 \div 2 =$ $8 \div 2 =$

$0 \div 9 =$ $7 \div 1 =$ $8 \div 4 =$ $4 \div 1 =$ $0 \div 7 =$

$6 \div 1 =$ $0 \div 5 =$ $8 \div 8 =$

Divide.

Name _____

$8 \div 1 =$ $4 \div 2 =$ $9 \div 9 =$ $7 \div 1 =$ $2 \div 2 =$

$1 \div 1 =$ $7 \div 7 =$ $0 \div 1 =$ $5 \div 5 =$ $0 \div 9 =$

$3 \div 3 =$ $4 \div 1 =$ $6 \div 2 =$ $6 \div 3 =$ $8 \div 8 =$

$7 \div 1 =$ $6 \div 6 =$ $2 \div 2 =$

Division

Name _____

Divide.

$7 \div 1 =$ $9 \div 9 =$ $0 \div 3 =$ $4 \div 2 =$ $8 \div 4 =$

$8 \div 2 =$ $6 \div 2 =$ $2 \div 2 =$ $9 \div 3 =$ $4 \div 1 =$

$8 \div 4 =$ $7 \div 7 =$ $0 \div 5 =$ $6 \div 3 =$ $5 \div 5 =$

$9 \div 1 =$ $6 \div 2 =$ $8 \div 4 =$

Divide.

Name _____

$9 \div 3 =$ $4 \div 4 =$ $1 \div 1 =$ $0 \div 5 =$ $6 \div 2 =$

$7 \div 7 =$ $6 \div 3 =$ $8 \div 2 =$ $6 \div 6 =$ $2 \div 2 =$

$0 \div 1 =$ $7 \div 1 =$ $6 \div 1 =$ $4 \div 2 =$ $8 \div 4 =$

$9 \div 3 =$ $0 \div 7 =$ $6 \div 6 =$

Name _____

Divide.

$6 \div 2 =$ $0 \div 4 =$ $9 \div 3 =$ $0 \div 8 =$ $4 \div 4 =$

$6 \div 3 =$ $7 \div 1 =$ $0 \div 1 =$ $5 \div 5 =$ $6 \div 1 =$

$7 \div 7 =$ $0 \div 5 =$ $8 \div 4 =$ $2 \div 2 =$ $9 \div 3 =$

$6 \div 3 =$ $0 \div 0 =$ $4 \div 1 =$

Divide.

Division

Name _____

$7 \div 1 =$ $8 \div 2 =$ $4 \div 4 =$ $0 \div 1 =$ $9 \div 3 =$

$6 \div 3 =$ $9 \div 9 =$ $1 \div 1 =$ $4 \div 2 =$ $8 \div 1 =$

$5 \div 5 =$ $8 \div 1 =$ $7 \div 7 =$ $0 \div 6 =$ $6 \div 3 =$

$0 \div 1 =$ $0 \div 4 =$ $8 \div 4 =$

Divide.

Division

Name _____

$9 \div 3 =$ $8 \div 4 =$ $4 \div 4 =$ $0 \div 1 =$ $7 \div 7 =$

$2\overline{)8}$ $9\overline{)9}$ $1\overline{)7}$ $3\overline{)6}$ $4\overline{)0}$ $6\overline{)6}$

$8 \div 4 =$ $9 \div 3 =$ $0 \div 9 =$ $4 \div 1 =$ $0 \div 6 =$

$2\overline{)4}$ $2\overline{)8}$ $4\overline{)4}$ $3\overline{)9}$

Divide.

Name _____

$8 \div 1 =$ $9 \div 3 =$ $6 \div 6 =$ $7 \div 7 =$ $0 \div 4 =$

$2\overline{)4}$ $2\overline{)8}$ $3\overline{)6}$ $1\overline{)9}$ $5\overline{)5}$ $2\overline{)6}$

$4 \div 2 =$ $4 \div 1 =$ $9 \div 9 =$ $1 \div 1 =$ $0 \div 7 =$

$1\overline{)0}$ $8\overline{)8}$ $2\overline{)0}$ $3\overline{)6}$

Division Word Problems

Solve each problem.

Name _____

Chris has 9 presents.

He gives them all to 3 friends.

How many presents did each get?

$$\begin{array}{r} 3 \\ 3 \overline{)9} \end{array}$$

There are 8 students in the classroom.

They are separated into 2 groups.

How many students are in each group?

There are 6 chairs in the room.

They are moved into 3 rooms.

How many chairs are in each room?

Rachel has 8 dolls.

She gives them all to 4 friends.

How many dolls did each get?

Division Word Problems

Solve each problem.

Name _____

Amy hit 6 homeruns.

She hit in 3 games.

How many homeruns did she hit in each game?

Doug has 8 pencils.

He gives them to 2 friends.

How many pencils does each friend have?

Dennis has 2 presents.

He gives them to 2 friends.

How many presents did each get?

Betsy sees 8 birds.

They fly away in 2 groups.

How many birds were in each group?

Division Word Problems

Solve each problem.

Name _____

There are 4 students.

They split into 4 groups.

How many students are in each group?

There are 9 cars.

They break up into 3 groups.

How many cars are in each group?

There are 7 tourists.

They split up into 1 group.

How many tourists are in each group?

There are 6 runners.

They run in groups of 2 runners.

How many groups are there?

Division

Solve each problem.

Name _____

Grace has 6 dresses.

She gives them evenly to 2 friends.

How many dresses did each get?

Rachel has 9 cats.

She puts them in 3 rooms.

How many cats are in each room?

Matt drinks 4 glasses of milk a day.

He only drinks milk 2 times a day.

How many glasses does he drink at a time?

Eric plays 8 games a week.

He only plays games on 2 days.

How many games does he play each day?

Division

Solve each problem.

Name _____

There are 5 students.

They are split into 5 groups.

How many students are in each group?

There are 9 students.

John splits them in 3 groups.

How many students are in each group?

There are 6 rabbits.

Only 2 go into each rabbit hole.

How many rabbit holes are there?

There are 9 bees.

They fly to 9 flowers.

How many bees are there on each flower?

Division Word Problems

Solve each problem.

Name _____

Dennis has 8 presents.

He gives them to 2 friends.

How many presents did each receive?

Lori has 7 cards.

She puts them in 1 pile.

How many cards are in each pile?

Devon sees 6 kites.

They are in 2 groups.

How many kites are in each group?

Sam has 9 toys.

He puts them in 3 groups.

How many toys are in each group?

Divide.

Name _____

$7\overline{)49}$ $2\overline{)12}$ $5\overline{)10}$ $3\overline{)18}$ $5\overline{)15}$ $8\overline{)40}$

$5\overline{)50}$ $4\overline{)28}$ $9\overline{)81}$ $6\overline{)36}$ $4\overline{)32}$ $7\overline{)35}$

$1\overline{)18}$ $4\overline{)12}$ $7\overline{)49}$ $7\overline{)56}$ $9\overline{)54}$ $8\overline{)88}$

$2\overline{)46}$ $6\overline{)42}$ $5\overline{)25}$ $8\overline{)64}$

Divide.

Name _____

$2\overline{)4\ 6}$ $8\overline{)4\ 0}$ $6\overline{)3\ 6}$ $9\overline{)9\ 0}$ $7\overline{)2\ 1}$ $6\overline{)4\ 8}$

$1\overline{)9\ 9}$ $1\overline{)7\ 4}$ $7\overline{)5\ 6}$ $9\overline{)1\ 8}$ $8\overline{)7\ 2}$ $6\overline{)2\ 4}$

$2\overline{)1\ 2}$ $7\overline{)2\ 1}$ $8\overline{)4\ 8}$ $4\overline{)2\ 8}$ $8\overline{)1\ 6}$ $6\overline{)3\ 6}$

$5\overline{)3\ 0}$ $5\overline{)4\ 0}$ $3\overline{)1\ 8}$ $2\overline{)1\ 0}$

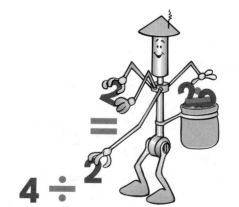

$4 \div 2$

Division

Divide.

Name _____

$1\overline{)1\,2}$ $5\overline{)4\,5}$ $8\overline{)7\,2}$ $7\overline{)4\,9}$ $9\overline{)7\,2}$ $6\overline{)3\,6}$

$5\overline{)2\,0}$ $8\overline{)1\,6}$ $8\overline{)4\,0}$ $2\overline{)5\,6}$ $6\overline{)5\,4}$ $3\overline{)2\,4}$

$2\overline{)3\,2}$ $7\overline{)6\,3}$ $5\overline{)4\,0}$ $1\overline{)4\,9}$ $8\overline{)4\,0}$ $2\overline{)1\,8}$

$3\overline{)1\,8}$ $1\overline{)2\,8}$ $9\overline{)8\,1}$ $7\overline{)1\,4}$

Division

Divide.

Name _____

$9\overline{)4\ 5}$ $6\overline{)4\ 2}$ $8\overline{)6\ 4}$ $9\overline{)5\ 4}$ $2\overline{)9\ 6}$ $6\overline{)4\ 8}$

$7\overline{)3\ 5}$ $7\overline{)6\ 3}$ $8\overline{)4\ 8}$ $6\overline{)4\ 8}$ $1\overline{)6\ 3}$ $7\overline{)2\ 1}$

$3\overline{)2\ 4}$ $6\overline{)1\ 8}$ $7\overline{)2\ 8}$ $3\overline{)3\ 9}$ $9\overline{)4\ 5}$ $7\overline{)5\ 6}$

$9\overline{)8\ 1}$ $1\overline{)4\ 6}$ $2\overline{)8\ 8}$ $7\overline{)1\ 4}$

86

Divide.

Name _____

$6\overline{)60}$ $9\overline{)81}$ $5\overline{)80}$ $1\overline{)16}$ $8\overline{)32}$ $6\overline{)18}$

$1\overline{)49}$ $6\overline{)48}$ $4\overline{)48}$ $5\overline{)45}$ $5\overline{)20}$ $2\overline{)44}$

$8\overline{)64}$ $3\overline{)18}$ $8\overline{)16}$ $4\overline{)32}$ $9\overline{)63}$ $2\overline{)18}$

$7\overline{)21}$ $2\overline{)56}$ $4\overline{)48}$ $2\overline{)14}$

Division

Divide.

Name _____

$3\overline{)18}$ $8\overline{)56}$ $5\overline{)45}$ $8\overline{)48}$ $8\overline{)72}$ $2\overline{)16}$

$6\overline{)36}$ $9\overline{)27}$ $6\overline{)30}$ $7\overline{)63}$ $3\overline{)18}$ $7\overline{)14}$

$5\overline{)20}$ $4\overline{)16}$ $7\overline{)42}$ $9\overline{)36}$ $8\overline{)40}$ $7\overline{)56}$

$7\overline{)42}$ $4\overline{)32}$ $8\overline{)16}$ $7\overline{)49}$

Division

Divide.

Name _____

$15 \div 5 =$ $27 \div 9 =$ $24 \div 6 =$ $56 \div 7 =$ $18 \div 2 =$

$24 \div 3 =$ $72 \div 9 =$ $25 \div 5 =$ $54 \div 6 =$ $32 \div 8 =$

$18 \div 9 =$ $36 \div 6 =$ $36 \div 1 =$ $91 \div 1 =$ $63 \div 9 =$

$10 \div 2 =$ $12 \div 3 =$ $24 \div 8 =$

Divide.

Name _____

30 ÷ 6 =   24 ÷ 3 =   24 ÷ 2 =   25 ÷ 5 =   16 ÷ 4 =

40 ÷ 8 =   36 ÷ 6 =   46 ÷ 1 =   14 ÷ 7 =   48 ÷ 2 =

72 ÷ 8 =   16 ÷ 8 =   72 ÷ 9 =   16 ÷ 8 =   15 ÷ 3 =

12 ÷ 4 =   15 ÷ 5 =   32 ÷ 4 =

Name _____

Divide.

$32 \div 4 =$ $18 \div 2 =$ $50 \div 2 =$ $25 \div 5 =$ $49 \div 7 =$

$27 \div 9 =$ $35 \div 7 =$ $19 \div 1 =$ $72 \div 9 =$ $27 \div 3 =$

$42 \div 7 =$ $36 \div 6 =$ $16 \div 8 =$ $36 \div 9 =$ $28 \div 7 =$

$14 \div 7 =$ $30 \div 5 =$ $21 \div 3 =$

Division

Divide.

Name _____

42 ÷ 7 =   12 ÷ 6 =   12 ÷ 3 =   28 ÷ 4 =   81 ÷ 9 =

56 ÷ 8 =   32 ÷ 8 =   40 ÷ 5 =   14 ÷ 2 =   30 ÷ 6 =

50 ÷ 5 =   63 ÷ 7 =   24 ÷ 4=   16 ÷ 4 =   32 ÷ 4 =

91 ÷ 1 =   36 ÷ 9 =   16 ÷ 2 =

Name _____

Divide.

$28 \div 4 =$ $24 \div 3 =$ $24 \div 4 =$ $56 \div 7 =$ $56 \div 4 =$

$15 \div 3 =$ $18 \div 9 =$ $12 \div 2 =$ $72 \div 9 =$ $32 \div 8 =$

$25 \div 5 =$ $27 \div 3 =$ $36 \div 6 =$ $72 \div 8 =$ $16 \div 2 =$

$49 \div 1 =$ $81 \div 9 =$ $64 \div 8 =$

Division

Divide.

Name _____

$35 \div 7 =$ $24 \div 3 =$ $25 \div 5 =$ $56 \div 7 =$ $45 \div 9 =$

$24 \div 8 =$ $63 \div 7 =$ $54 \div 6 =$ $72 \div 8 =$ $54 \div 9 =$

$64 \div 8 =$ $60 \div 5 =$ $24 \div 8 =$ $17 \div 1 =$ $0 \div 19 =$

$70 \div 7 =$ $88 \div 4 =$ $27 \div 9 =$

Name _____

Divide.

$36 \div 9 =$ $80 \div 8 =$ $46 \div 2 =$ $94 \div 1 =$ $36 \div 6 =$

$7\overline{)4\ 9}$ $8\overline{)4\ 0}$ $7\overline{)2\ 8}$ $1\overline{)2\ 8}$ $8\overline{)6\ 4}$ $7\overline{)2\ 1}$

$72 \div 9 =$ $35 \div 7 =$ $18 \div 6 =$ $24 \div 2 =$ $20 \div 5 =$

$2\overline{)1\ 0}$ $1\overline{)1\ 0}$ $3\overline{)2\ 4}$ $9\overline{)8\ 1}$

Divide.

Division

Name _____

12 ÷ 6 =   30 ÷ 6 =   27 ÷ 9 =   24 ÷ 8 =   54 ÷ 2 =

6)42   4)20   7)28   8)56   5)40   9)36

63 ÷ 9 =   72 ÷ 8 =   27 ÷ 3 =   28 ÷ 7 =   63 ÷ 7 =

6)48   7)14   8)32   5)45

Division

Solve each problem.

Name _____

There are 45 students.

They are put in 5 groups.

$$5\overline{)45} = 9$$

How many students are in each group?

Ken has 10 pencils.

He puts them in 2 groups.

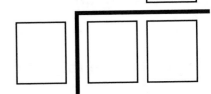

How many pencils are in each group?

Devon has 49 presents.

She gives them to 7 friends.

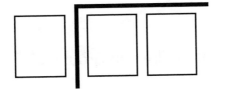

How many presents does each receive?

Greg has 99 balloons.

He puts them in 9 groups.

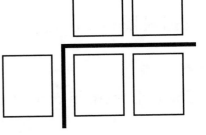

How many balloons are in each group?

Division Word Problems

Solve each problem.

Name _____

Chris has 48 eggs.

He puts them in rows of 6.

How many rows of eggs are there?

There are 60 students.

They are put in groups of 3.

How many groups are there?

Rachel has 81 ants.

She puts them in groups of 9.

How many groups are there?

Spencer sees 24 cars.

They drive in groups of 2.

How many groups are there?

Division Word Problems

Solve each problem.

Name _____

There are 64 chairs.

They are in 8 rows.

How many chairs are in each row?

Shirley has 28 balloons.

Each person gets 2 balloons.

How many people are there?

George has 18 birds.

He puts 2 birds in each cage.

How many cages does he have?

Debra has 38 apples.

She puts 2 in each bag.

How many bags does she have?

Division Word Problems

Solve each problem.

Name _____

Sam read 35 pages in his book.

It took him 7 days.

How many pages did he read each day?

Tammy worked 18 hours.

She worked for 2 days.

How many hours did she work each day?

Doug bought 54 cards.

They came in 6 boxes.

How many cards are in each box?

A basketball game is 32 minutes long.

The game is split in 4 parts.

How long is each part?

Division

Solve each problem.

Name _____

Amy worked 49 problems.

She did 7 problems per page.

How many pages did she use?

A team played 48 quarters.

There are 4 quarters a game.

How many games did they play?

There are 20 slices of bread in a loaf.

George uses 5 slices a day.

How many days will the loaf last?

Keith has 10 books.

He puts them in 2 stacks.

How many books are in each stack?

Division Word Problems

Solve each problem.

Name _____

Tom has 88 inches of wire.

He cuts it in 4 pieces.

How many inches are each piece?

Barb has 28 cats.

They play in groups of 2.

How many cats are in each group?

Emily got 18 hits.

She played 3 games.

How many hits did she get in each game?

A movie was shown 30 times.

It was shown for 5 days.

How many times was the movie shown each day?

Divide.

Name _____

8 ÷ 2 =   32 ÷ 8 =   49 ÷ 7 =   72 ÷ 9 =   50 ÷ 5 =

2)4 8   1)9   9)4 5   9)0   8)4 8   2)4

81 ÷ 9 =   7 ÷ 7 =   12 ÷ 3 =   6 ÷ 2 =   32 ÷ 4 =

4)4   5)1 5   1)8   5)2 0

Divide

Divide.

Name _____

$2 \div 2 =$ 　　　　 $12 \div 1 =$ 　　　　 $9 \div 3 =$ 　　　　 $40 \div 5 =$ 　　　　 $6 \div 2 =$

$6\overline{)30}$ 　　　 $2\overline{)8}$ 　　　 $6\overline{)42}$ 　　　 $1\overline{)8}$ 　　　 $7\overline{)35}$ 　　　 $2\overline{)6}$

$56 \div 7 =$ 　　　　 $8 \div 4 =$ 　　　　 $14 \div 2 =$ 　　　　 $8 \div 8 =$ 　　　　 $72 \div 8 =$

$1\overline{)9}$ 　　　 $9\overline{)54}$ 　　　 $2\overline{)6}$ 　　　 $7\overline{)63}$

Division Review

Divide.

Divide

Name _____

$8 \div 4 =$ $21 \div 7 =$ $8 \div 8 =$ $72 \div 9 =$ $6 \div 2 =$

$5\overline{)2\ 5}$ $3\overline{)6}$ $3\overline{)1\ 8}$ $1\overline{)9}$ $8\overline{)5\ 6}$ $8\overline{)8}$

$56 \div 7 =$ $9 \div 1 =$ $24 \div 8 =$ $7 \div 7 =$ $21 \div 7 =$

$9\overline{)0}$ $6\overline{)4\ 2}$ $5\overline{)5}$ $6\overline{)1\ 2}$

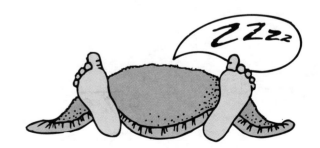

Division Review

Divide.

$4 \div 4 =$ $28 \div 2 =$ $6 \div 3 =$ $72 \div 8 =$ $9 \div 9 =$

$3\overline{)2\ 4}$ $7\overline{)0}$ $8\overline{)4\ 8}$ $7\overline{)7}$ $6\overline{)3\ 6}$ $5\overline{)5}$

$40 \div 8 =$ $8 \div 4 =$ $19 \div 1 =$ $2 \div 2 =$ $45 \div 9 =$

$1\overline{)9}$ $9\overline{)7\ 2}$ $6\overline{)6}$ $7\overline{)6\ 3}$

Divide.

Name _____

$7 \div 7 =$

$42 \div 7 =$

$5 \div 5 =$

$56 \div 8 =$

$8 \div 2 =$

$5\overline{)2\ 0}$

$2\overline{)8}$

$8\overline{)4\ 8}$

$3\overline{)9}$

$2\overline{)4\ 8}$

$6\overline{)0}$

$28 \div 7 =$

$1 \div 1 =$

$27 \div 9 =$

$0 \div 8 =$

$63 \div 9 =$

$2\overline{)6}$

$8\overline{)4\ 0}$

$5\overline{)5}$

$6\overline{)3\ 6}$

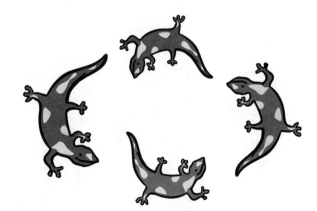

Division Review

Divide.

Name _____

$6 \div 6 =$ $42 \div 6 =$ $0 \div 7 =$ $11 \div 1 =$ $8 \div 4 =$

$2\overline{)4\ 8}$ $6\overline{)0}$ $7\overline{)6\ 3}$ $8\overline{)8}$ $4\overline{)2\ 8}$ $9\overline{)9}$

$54 \div 2 =$ $9 \div 3 =$ $18 \div 9 =$ $6 \div 1 =$ $42 \div 6 =$

$7\overline{)7}$ $8\overline{)1\ 6}$ $5\overline{)0}$ $8\overline{)4\ 0}$

Divide.

Name _____

$6 \div 2 =$ $21 \div 7 =$ $4 \div 1 =$ $54 \div 6 =$ $0 \div 8 =$

$7\overline{\smash{)}3\ 5}$ $9\overline{\smash{)}9}$ $8\overline{\smash{)}6\ 4}$ $1\overline{\smash{)}0}$ $6\overline{\smash{)}1\ 8}$ $3\overline{\smash{)}6}$

$14 \div 2 =$ $9 \div 1 =$ $72 \div 8 =$ $8 \div 2 =$ $42 \div 7 =$

$2\overline{\smash{)}4}$ $2\overline{\smash{)}4\ 4}$ $1\overline{\smash{)}8}$ $4\overline{\smash{)}4\ 8}$

Division Review

Divide.

$7 \div 7 =$ $24 \div 6 =$ $8 \div 1 =$ $56 \div 7 =$ $0 \div 5 =$

$6\overline{)3\ 0}$ $6\overline{)6}$ $1\overline{)9\ 9}$ $7\overline{)0}$ $9\overline{)6\ 3}$ $2\overline{)8}$

$36 \div 6 =$ $9 \div 3 =$ $85 \div 5 =$ $8 \div 4 =$ $21 \div 7 =$

$2\overline{)4}$ $2\overline{)1\ 4}$ $4\overline{)4}$ $9\overline{)1\ 8}$

$8\overline{)48}$

Divide.

Name _____

$2 \div 2 =$ $32 \div 8 =$ $1 \div 1 =$ $24 \div 6 =$ $8 \div 4 =$

$6\overline{)3\ 6}$ $5\overline{)0}$ $4\overline{)3\ 2}$ $9\overline{)9}$ $9\overline{)5\ 4}$ $5\overline{)5}$

$10 \div 5 =$ $4 \div 1 =$ $24 \div 3 =$ $9 \div 3 =$ $81 \div 9 =$

$7\overline{)0}$ $2\overline{)1\ 4}$ $1\overline{)3}$ $4\overline{)2\ 0}$

$9\overline{)72}$

Division Review

Divide.

Name _____

$4 \div 1 =$ $28 \div 4 =$ $9 \div 9 =$ $45 \div 5 =$ $8 \div 4 =$

$1\overline{)1\ 8}$ $3\overline{)6}$ $9\overline{)3\ 6}$ $2\overline{)8}$ $4\overline{)1\ 6}$ $1\overline{)0}$

$20 \div 5 =$ $9 \div 1 =$ $36 \div 6 =$ $6 \div 2 =$ $49 \div 7 =$

$2\overline{)4}$ $2\overline{)4\ 8}$ $1\overline{)9}$ $6\overline{)1\ 2}$

Divide

Divide.

Name _____

$8 \div 2 =$ $\qquad$ $40 \div 5 =$ $\qquad$ $9 \div 3 =$ $\qquad$ $36 \div 4 =$ $\qquad$ $7 \div 1 =$

$1 \overline{)1\ 2}$ $\qquad$ $2 \overline{)6}$ $\qquad$ $7 \overline{)4\ 9}$ $\qquad$ $4 \overline{)4}$ $\qquad$ $5 \overline{)1\ 5}$ $\qquad$ $9 \overline{)0}$

$28 \div 4 =$ $\qquad$ $4 \div 1 =$ $\qquad$ $40 \div 8 =$ $\qquad$ $8 \div 8 =$ $\qquad$ $81 \div 9 =$

$7 \overline{)7}$ $\qquad$ $7 \overline{)5\ 6}$ $\qquad$ $6 \overline{)0}$ $\qquad$ $5 \overline{)8\ 5}$

Divide

Divide.

Name _____

7 ÷ 7 =   12 ÷ 6 =   64 ÷ 8 =   0 ÷ 1 =   45 ÷ 9 =

7⟌2̄8̄   3⟌6̄   4⟌3̄2̄   4⟌4̄   3⟌1̄2̄   1⟌3̄

27 ÷ 3 =   8 ÷ 4 =   35 ÷ 7 =   9 ÷ 1 =   72 ÷ 8 =

5⟌0̄   6⟌2̄4̄   1⟌7̄   6⟌4̄2̄

Divide.

Divide

Name _____

$9 \div 1 =$ $48 \div 8 =$ $0 \div 5 =$ $10 \div 5 =$ $6 \div 2 =$

$6\overline{)5\ 4}$ $2\overline{)8}$ $7\overline{)6\ 3}$ $1\overline{)9}$ $7\overline{)4\ 9}$ $3\overline{)6}$

$81 \div 9 =$ $7 \div 7 =$ $40 \div 8 =$ $8 \div 1 =$ $56 \div 8 =$

$5\overline{)5}$ $9\overline{)1\ 8}$ $3\overline{)9}$ $8\overline{)6\ 4}$

Divide. | Divide

Name _____

6 ÷ 1 =   36 ÷ 6 =   8 ÷ 2 =   45 ÷ 9 =   2 ÷ 2 =

8)5 6   7)0   6)5 4   4)8   5)3 0   1)6

48 ÷ 4 =   6 ÷ 2 =   10 ÷ 5 =   4 ÷ 2 =   40 ÷ 5 =

4)0   2)1 2   3)6   7)4 9

Division Word Problems Review

Divide

Solve each problem.

There are 9 students.

They are split into 3 groups.

$$3\overline{)9}$$ 3

How many students are in each group?

There are 25 eggs.

Chris puts them in groups of 5.

How many groups of eggs are there?

There are 17 cats.

They are split into 1 group.

How many cats are in the group?

There are 6 cars in the parking lot.

They are in 3 rows.

How many cars are in each row?

Division Word Problems Review

Divide

Solve each problem.

Name _____

There are 8 pencils in a package.

They are in 2 rows in the package.

How many pencils are in each row?

Dorothy has 84 balloons.

She gives 4 to each person.

How many people are there?

Eric has 36 books.

He puts them on 6 shelves.

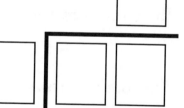
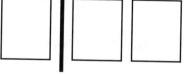

How many books are there on each shelf?

Orson sees 8 birds.

They are flying in groups of 4.

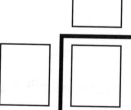

How many groups of birds are there?

Solve each problem.

Name _____

Colin has 6 cards.

He puts them in groups of 3.

How many groups of cards are there?

There are 99 plants in a garden.

They are planted in rows of 9.

How many rows of plants are there?

There are 63 students.

They are put in groups of 7.

How many groups are there?

There are 5 posters on the wall.

They are put in 1 row.

How many posters are in the row?

Division Word Problems Review

Divide ÷

Solve each problem.

Name _____

There are 9 chairs.

They are in rows of 3 chairs.

How many rows are there?

Beth has 85 quarters.

She puts them in stacks of 5.

How many stacks of quarters does she have?

Lindsay has 64 shirts.

She hangs them in 2 closets.

How many shirts are in each closet?

There are 4 chairs.

They are put on 2 sides of the table.

How many chairs are on each side of the table?

Division Word Problems Review

Divide ÷

Name _____

Solve each problem.

Emily hit 9 homeruns.

She hit them in 3 games.

How many homeruns did she hit in each game?

Greg ran 20 miles today.

He only ran 5 miles at a time.

How many different times did he run today?

There are 56 runners.

They run in 7 groups.

How many runners were in each group?

There are 8 tourists.

They are in 8 groups.

How many tourists are in each group?

Divide

÷

Solve each problem.

Name _____

There are 6 students.

They are in groups of 3 students.

How many groups are there?

There are 20 cars on the highway.

They are driving in 4 lanes.

How many cars are in each lane?

Devon sees 77 stars in the sky.

They are in 7 groups.

How many stars are in each group?

David has 8 toys.

He puts them in 4 boxes.

How many toys are in each box?

Answer Key

Page 4
15 28   2 35 64 72
15 42   1 28 32 35
 0 40 48 49

Page 5
20   2 24 63 54   0
56   8 40 12 24 18
49 45 40   9

Page 6
12 28 35   0 40 14
42 40 10 81 24 36
 0 15   5 63

Page 7
 8 35 48 63   0 18
35   7 30   0 49 24
21   6 12 15

Page 8
24 35 24 48 81   0
28 40 24 28 36 20
 0 15   1   8

Page 9
 5 15 49 40   9
24 35   8   1 54
 3   9 40 28 25
36 28 24

Page 10
15   2 24 30 18
36 28   8 12 40
16   0 49   0   9
27 35 16

Page 11
 2 16 35   0 24
 1   0   6 49 40
 8 40 36 15 24
36 25   0

Page 12
32 48 21   0   6
15 12   8 35 49
45 56 32 28 25
 0   4 18

Page 13
32 21 45 42   2
 9   0 24 16 64
 1 18   0 63 14
36 25   0

Page 14
 1   0 16 24 35
32 14 12   0   8
28   9 54 25 18
 7 21   0

Page 15
15 72   0 28 0
21 49 32 45 9 54
 5 24 16

Page 16
18 27 49 45 0
21 64 28 72 0 25
 1 42 40

Page 17

$$
\begin{array}{cccc}
2 & 4 & 1 & 2 \\
\times 3 & \times 2 & \times 9 & \times 3 \\
\hline
6 & 8 & 9 & 6
\end{array}
$$

Page 18

$$
\begin{array}{cccc}
7 & 4 & 2 & 8 \\
\times 2 & \times 2 & \times 3 & \times 3 \\
\hline
14 & 8 & 6 & 24
\end{array}
$$

Page 19

$$
\begin{array}{cccc}
3 & 2 & 8 & 3 \\
\times 3 & \times 4 & \times 1 & \times 2 \\
\hline
9 & 8 & 8 & 6
\end{array}
$$

Page 20

$$
\begin{array}{cccc}
4 & 5 & 4 & 8 \\
\times 7 & \times 5 & \times 2 & \times 3 \\
\hline
28 & 25 & 8 & 24
\end{array}
$$

Page 21

$$
\begin{array}{cccc}
3 & 7 & 2 & 2 \\
\times 2 & \times 2 & \times 4 & \times 8 \\
\hline
6 & 14 & 8 & 16
\end{array}
$$

Page 22

$$
\begin{array}{cccc}
5 & 2 & 2 & 2 \\
\times 8 & \times 7 & \times 2 & \times 3 \\
\hline
40 & 14 & 4 & 6
\end{array}
$$

Page 23
512 182   0   65 252 68
140   72 592 220 450 90
420 378 105   0

Page 24
146 140 204   50 294 288
315 147 420 228 192 248
 32 315   11 512

Answer Key

Page 25
260 73 252 86 350 92
106 510 168 190 74 252
155 63 301 300

Page 26
365 70 77 252 672 294
320 238 585 360 224 518
78 371 370 0

Page 27
252 32 376 333 510 448
224 102 450 84 370 85
448 294 225 95

Page 28
224 370 83 294 240 91
33 0 235 664 294 158
512 186 340 43

Page 29
56 120 228 496 0
52 582 95 399 248
243 144 82 90 430
420 174 304

Page 30
25 300 553 39 624
83 0 376 30 637
60 82 152 0 174
608 322 294

Page 31
336 174 368 0 288
22 171 114 30 510
498 177 82 195 60
44 165 855

Page 32
37 84 483 384 92
581 240 132 60 248
90 118 215 146 10
340 0 70

Page 33
48 415 370 0 108
456 96 581 525 392
110 264 0 24 736
184 532 672

Page 34
388 372 70 228 365
19 132 0 490 144
72 301 343 165 75
378 432 288

Page 35
201 95 441 76 196
180 95 300 42 156 0
456 236 43

Page 36
84 116 0 399 99
423 78 128 0 364 98
332 140 344

Page 37

$$\begin{array}{cccc} 39 & 29 & 11 & 32 \\ \times\ 2 & \times\ 8 & \times\ 5 & \times\ 2 \\ \hline 78 & 232 & 55 & 64 \end{array}$$

Page 38

$$\begin{array}{cccc} 14 & 42 & 50 & 13 \\ \times\ 5 & \times\ 3 & \times\ 7 & \times\ 4 \\ \hline 70 & 126 & 350 & 52 \end{array}$$

Page 39

$$\begin{array}{cccc} 14 & 37 & 41 & 12 \\ \times\ 8 & \times\ 7 & \times\ 2 & \times\ 3 \\ \hline 112 & 259 & 82 & 36 \end{array}$$

Page 40

$$\begin{array}{cccc} 19 & 41 & 31 & 10 \\ \times\ 3 & \times\ 5 & \times\ 6 & \times\ 2 \\ \hline 57 & 205 & 186 & 20 \end{array}$$

Page 41

$$\begin{array}{cccc} 10 & 28 & 29 & 12 \\ \times\ 5 & \times\ 1 & \times\ 7 & \times\ 4 \\ \hline 50 & 28 & 203 & 48 \end{array}$$

Page 42

$$\begin{array}{cccc} 47 & 11 & 23 & 72 \\ \times\ 2 & \times\ 2 & \times\ 3 & \times\ 2 \\ \hline 94 & 22 & 69 & 144 \end{array}$$

Page 43
420 7 0 35 427
144 1 222 54 42 40
12 188 35

Page 44
285 0 38 32 546
375 21 108 28 288 0
81 67 40

Page 45
282 14 282 18 441
175 0 25 24 54 48
8 246 6

Answer Key

Page 46
175 12 57 72 252
  0 24 201 16 301 8
 36 430 21

Page 47
380 42 413 5 504
 79 28 148 24 371 0
 24 348 5

Page 48
177 14 228 8 558
185 14 444 10 370 9
  0 108 12

Page 49
153 40 96 7 340
282 0 45 28 592 54
 21 117 21

Page 50
95 56 28 28 0
60 18 592 0 185 7
30 441 21

Page 51
355 49 387 32 688
144 8 456 0 148 36
  8 219 16

Page 52
 76 16 203 24 574
456 0 185 8 344 72
 35 56 49

Page 53
192 21 72 81 294
441 40 88 32 162 12
  0 58 56

Page 54
 85 49 252 129 106
371 24 390 40 180 32
  5 455 49

Page 55
73 0 513 42 86
64 32 756 0 185 72
 8 114 24

Page 56
 59 12 592 21 0
185 56 204 18 0 40
  7 335 0

Page 57

2	36	13	5
× 3	× 2	× 5	× 2
6	72	65	10

Page 58

2	47	87	4
× 8	× 8	× 7	× 1
16	376	609	4

Page 59

3	58	10	4
× 3	× 5	× 6	× 2
9	290	60	8

Page 60

9	73	28	4
× 0	× 4	× 3	× 1
0	292	84	4

Page 61

2	12	15	4
× 7	× 3	× 6	× 3
14	36	90	12

Page 62

2	99	38	4
× 1	× 4	× 3	× 2
2	396	114	8

Page 64
3 3 9 2 7 4
4 2 8 3 5 2
2 1 1 7 1 3
4 3 3 2

Page 65
2 1 0 2 7 3
1 1 7 1 2 1
5 2 1 1 8 1
2 6 2 4

Page 66
4 4 1 2 0 1
2 8 3 1 6 2
1 1 1 3 3 1
4 2 1 0

Answer Key

Page 67
9 1 1 2 4 7
2 2 5 1 1 1
5 2 1 0 2 3
4 0 1 2

Page 68
1 0 2 3 4 3
1 1 7 1 0 5
4 2 2 4 1 1
8 1 2 2

Page 69
1 4 9 0 2
1 2 1 3 4
0 7 2 4 0
6 0 1

Page 70
8 2 1 7 1
1 1 0 1 0
1 4 3 2 1
7 1 1

Page 71
7 1 0 2 2
4 3 1 3 4
2 1 0 2 1
9 3 2

Page 72
3 1 1 0 3
1 2 4 1 1
0 7 6 2 2
3 0 1

Page 73
3 0 3 0 1
2 7 0 1 6
1 0 2 1 3
2 0 4

Page 74
7 4 1 0 3
2 1 1 2 8
1 8 1 0 2
0 0 2

Page 75
3 2 1 0 1
4 1 7 2 0 1
2 3 0 4 0
2 4 1 3

Page 76
8 3 1 1 0
2 4 2 9 1 3
2 4 1 1 0
0 1 0 2

Page 77

$3\overline{)9}=3$ $2\overline{)8}=4$ $3\overline{)6}=2$ $4\overline{)8}=2$

Page 78

$3\overline{)6}=2$ $2\overline{)8}=4$ $2\overline{)2}=1$ $2\overline{)8}=4$

Page 79

$4\overline{)4}=1$ $3\overline{)9}=3$ $1\overline{)7}=7$ $2\overline{)6}=3$

Page 80

$2\overline{)6}=3$ $3\overline{)9}=3$ $2\overline{)4}=2$ $2\overline{)8}=4$

Page 81

$5\overline{)5}=1$ $3\overline{)9}=3$ $2\overline{)6}=3$ $9\overline{)9}=1$

Page 82

$2\overline{)8}=4$ $1\overline{)7}=7$ $2\overline{)6}=3$ $3\overline{)9}=3$

Page 83
7 6 2 6 3 5
10 7 9 6 8 5
18 3 7 8 6 11
23 7 5 8

Page 84
23 5 6 10 3 8
99 74 8 2 9 4
6 3 6 7 2 6
6 8 6 5

Page 85
12 9 9 7 8 6
4 2 5 28 9 8
16 9 8 49 5 9
6 28 9 2

Page 86
5 7 8 6 48 8
5 9 6 8 63 3
8 3 4 13 5 8
9 46 44 2

Page 87
10 9 16 16 4 3
49 8 12 9 4 22
8 6 2 8 7 9
3 28 12 7

Page 88
6 7 9 6 9 8
6 3 5 9 6 2
4 4 6 4 5 8
6 8 2 7

Page 89
3 3   4   8 9
8 8   5   9 4
2 6 36 91 7
5 4   3

Page 90
5 8 12 5   4
5 6 46 2 24
9 2 8 2   5
3 3 8

Page 91
8 9 25 5 7
3 5 19 8 9
6 6   2 4 4
2 6   7

Page 92
6 2 4 7 9
7 4 8 7 5
10 9 6 4 8
91 4 8

Page 93
7 8 6 8 14
5 2 6 8 4
5 9 6 9 8
49 9 8

Page 94
5 8 5 8 5
3 9 9 9 6
8 12 3 17 0
10 22 3

Page 95
4 10 23 94 6
7 5 4 28 8 3
8 5 3 12 4
5 10 8 9

Page 96
2 5 3 3 27
7 5 4 7 8 4
7 9 9 4 9
8 2 4 9

Page 97
$\frac{9}{5\overline{)45}}$ $\frac{5}{2\overline{)10}}$ $\frac{7}{7\overline{)49}}$ $\frac{11}{9\overline{)99}}$

Page 98
$\frac{8}{6\overline{)48}}$ $\frac{20}{3\overline{)60}}$ $\frac{9}{9\overline{)81}}$ $\frac{12}{2\overline{)24}}$

Page 99
$\frac{8}{8\overline{)64}}$ $\frac{14}{2\overline{)28}}$ $\frac{9}{2\overline{)18}}$ $\frac{19}{2\overline{)38}}$

Page 100
$\frac{5}{7\overline{)35}}$ $\frac{9}{2\overline{)18}}$ $\frac{9}{6\overline{)54}}$ $\frac{8}{4\overline{)32}}$

Page 101
$\frac{7}{7\overline{)49}}$ $\frac{12}{4\overline{)48}}$ $\frac{4}{5\overline{)20}}$ $\frac{5}{2\overline{)10}}$

Page 102
$\frac{22}{4\overline{)88}}$ $\frac{14}{2\overline{)28}}$ $\frac{6}{3\overline{)18}}$ $\frac{6}{5\overline{)30}}$

Page 103
4 4 7 8 10
24 9 5 0 6 2
9 1 4 3 8
1 3 8 4

Page 104
1 12 3 8 3
5 4 7 8 5 3
8 2 7 1 9
9 6 3 9

Page 105
2 3 1 8 3
5 2 6 9 7 1
8 9 3 1 3
0 7 1 2

Page 106
1 14 2 9 1
8 0 6 1 6 1
5 2 19 1 5
9 8 1 9

Page 107
1 6 1 7 4
4 4 6 3 24 0
4 1 3 0 7
3 5 1 6

Page 108
1 7 0 11 2
24 0 9 1 7 1
27 3 2 6 7
1 2 0 5

Page 109

3 3 4 90
5 18 0 32
7 99 46
2 22 8 12

Page 110

14 880
5 1 99 0 74
6 3 17 23
27 12

Page 111

14 142
60 8 161
24 839
07 35

Page 112

4 7 1 92
18 2 44 0
4 9 637
2 24 92

Page 113

48 3 97
12 37 130
74 5 19
18 0 17

Page 114

12 805
4 28 143
92 599
0 477

Page 115

96 023
9 4 99 72
9 1 587
1 238

Page 116

66 451
70 9 266
12 3 228
06 27

Page 117

$3\overline{)9}$ = 3 $5\overline{)25}$ = 5 $1\overline{)17}$ = 17 $3\overline{)6}$ = 2

Page 118

$2\overline{)8}$ = 4 $4\overline{)84}$ = 21 $6\overline{)36}$ = 6 $4\overline{)8}$ = 2

Page 119

$3\overline{)6}$ = 2 $9\overline{)99}$ = 11 $7\overline{)63}$ = 9 $1\overline{)5}$ = 5

Page 120

$3\overline{)9}$ = 3 $5\overline{)85}$ = 17 $2\overline{)64}$ = 32 $2\overline{)4}$ = 2

Page 121

$3\overline{)9}$ = 3 $5\overline{)20}$ = 4 $7\overline{)56}$ = 8 $8\overline{)8}$ = 1

Page 122

$3\overline{)6}$ = 2 $4\overline{)20}$ = 5 $7\overline{)77}$ = 11 $4\overline{)8}$ = 2